THIS BOOK WILL HOPEFULLY HELP YOU ORGANIZE THE THINGS YOU COLLECT. IT CAN BE THE PLACE TO PUT LEAVES YOU ARE FLATTENING OUT, NEWSPAPER PICTURES YOU WANT TO SAVE FOR DRAWING OR JUST LOOKING AT LATER, RECEIPTS FROM DINNERS YOU WANT TO REMEMBER, OR REALLY ANYTHING ELSE YOU CAN THINK OF (THAT IS MOSTLY FLAT). WE HOPE YOU ENJOY FILLING IT UP.

 CONTAINER

 BIGGER
CONTAINER

NET

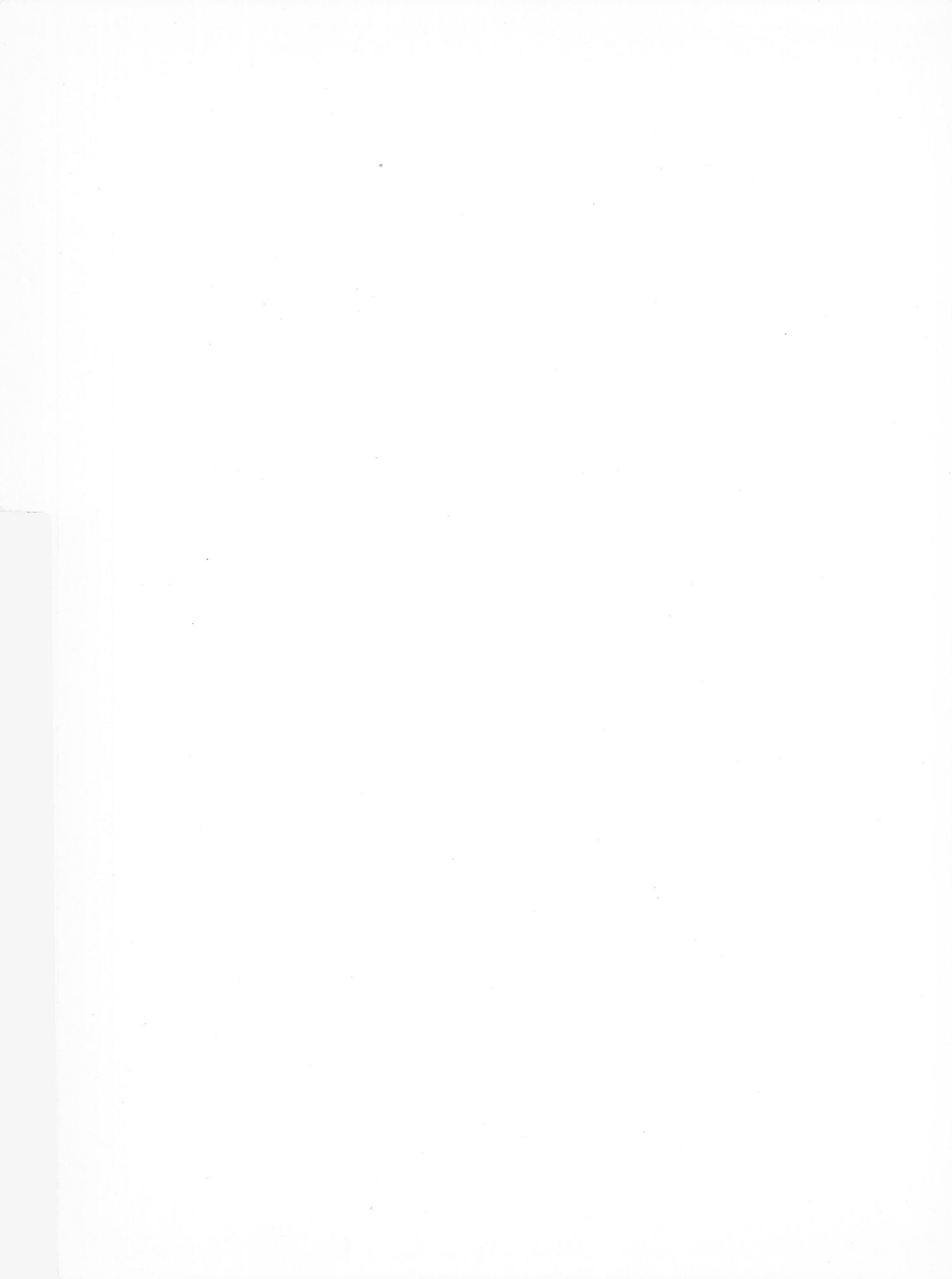

JAR
WITH HOLES
PUNCHED IN
TOP

PUSH PIN

TRAFFIC
CONE

Artwork © Jason Polan
Journal © 2014 Who's There Inc.

Developed by Tucker Nichols
Designed by MacFadden & Thorpe

Made in China / Fabriqué en Chine /
Hecho en China

Distributed by / Distribué par /
Distribuido por
Who's There Inc. Venice, CA 90291

UPC: 825703-31013-9
ISBN: 978-160106637-4

10 9 8 7 6 5 4 3 2 1

plumbgoods.com

POMEGRANATE

DUCK EGG

TRUMPET ROYALE MUSHROOM

PERSIMMON

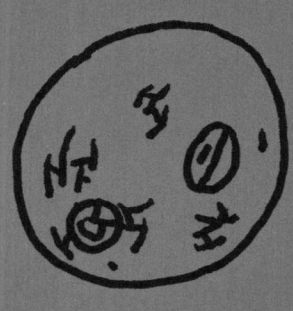
CANTALOUPE

MUENSTER CHEESE

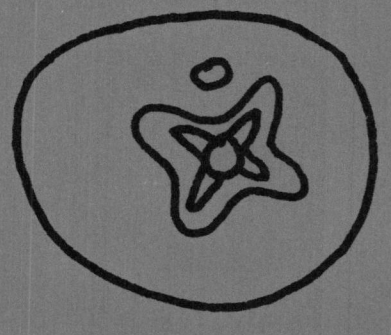
POMELO WITH A BIG STICKER ON It

THREE BRUSSELS SPROUTS

HARD-BOILED EGG

POTATO

EARPLUG

PUMPKIN

WHIPPED CREAM